To Trey –
With all my love
and thanks for being a
wonderful friend – to me
and to my beloved Becky –
Name

9/10/08

# Shopping for Love

# Shopping for Love

Rachel Levy Lesser

Library of Congress Control Number:    2008904750
ISBN:            Hardcover              978-1-4363-4665-8
                 Softcover              978-1-4363-4664-1

**To order additional copies of this book, contact:**
Xlibris Corporation
1-888-795-4274
www.Xlibris.com
Orders@Xlibris.com
50156

# DEDICATION

For my mother, Becky Deitz Levy,
who always did the right thing

# PREFACE

I HAD NO choice but to shop. My maternal grandparents, Helene and Joe Deitz, known affectionately by their grandchildren as Madee and Padee, were shoppers. Some people play golf or tennis, ski, read, or watch sports. My grandparents shopped. When traveling through London, they always went to Harrods and headed straight to Galeries Lafayette while in Paris. If visiting friends in Fort Worth, they would make a special trip to Neiman Marcus in Dallas. And when my grandfather, at the age of ninety-three, just three months before he died, visited my cousin in Portland, Oregon, he made a special trip to see the original Nordstrom in that city. I remember one day, when I was home from school over Thanksgiving break, I had mentioned to Madee that I lost the button to my toggle coat while at a football game. She set up a special shopping day based on the premise of finding that perfect button.

Shopping was something that my family did, but we most certainly kept it in perspective. I say that we shopped, but of course, we did other things. We read, worked hard in school and got good jobs, went to museums, played sports, volunteered, traveled, and much more. Growing up, I was instilled with valuing education, family, friendship, and the simple things in life. My mother, Becky, always told me that I was "rich with love," and that was all that mattered. I later discovered that we were lucky enough to shop without worrying about it too much. And that was that.

Let me explain the history of the real shoppers in my family. My grandmother, Madee, was an only child who grew into a beautiful and elegant woman. She was the Audrey Hepburn type, always put together, but she never overdid it. A paper bag could look good on her. She married Padee and became the mother of two girls, Joanne and Becky. Two girls were all that Madee needed to keep up with her shopping habit. When Joanne and Becky recount their childhood, they can tell you exactly where their mother bought them each outfit. They were clearly taught how to shop and how to do it well.

Joanne, the elder of the two is my aunt (Aunt Jo). She was very much the spitting image of the beautiful and elegant Madee. Joanne picked up Madee's tricks and trades, and she became a great, stylish, and decisive shopper. Like Madee, she was always put together, but she added funky elements to her look that would never work for Madee.

The baby sister, Becky (my mother), on the other hand, was like her father in every way. She was more of the tomboy. Mommy loved to play sports and could not dress herself if her life depended on it. This, however, did not preclude her from becoming a shopper and always looking great. She simply never shopped alone. Madee and Aunt Jo were always by her side telling her what to wear so that in her own Becky way, she looked completely adorable.

Joanne and Becky grew up, got married, and had children of their own. Aunt Jo first had two boys, followed by my mother, who had one boy and then a girl—me. When my mother was pregnant with me (back in the days before amnios and ultrasounds), Madee, knowing that this would be the last chance for her to have a granddaughter, asked my mother if this new child could get its ears pierced regardless of its gender so that it could wear all her beautiful earrings that she had so lovingly shopped for all of those years.

Just hours after I was born, while my mother sat drugged out in the hospital in Philadelphia, Madee and Aunt Jo went to the Children's Boutique and bought everything in the store that was pink.

It was in the stars: Madee, Aunt Jo, Mommy, and I would shop for many years and for many reasons—just because, to be together, to find the perfect dress for some occasion, for fun, for distractions, for ourselves, for each other, for hope, for love.

# CHAPTER 1

MY MOTHER NEVER bought any clothes for me until I was eighteen years old. That is because Madee always did. As the only granddaughter of the shopping maven, I got everything brand new. My brother, on the other hand, wore all hand-me-downs from our older cousins. When my grandmother bought him a brand-new blue blazer to wear to his bar mitzvah, he could not understand where it came from. Who had worn it before? What were those tags hanging off it?

❧

I was five years old when Madee took me to buy a dress for my consecration (a Jewish ceremony that signifies the beginning of a child's religious school experience.) We went to Bello's, a women and children's boutique in Princeton, New Jersey, right near where we lived. I grasped Madee's hand tightly as we crossed the busy street to get to the store. As young children often do, I tried to walk briskly across the street as Madee's calm and cool hand held me back. I can still feel myself turning the rings around her finger—a nervous habit of mine that she did not like.

Madee was usually pretty definite about which dresses I could get. However, on this day, I was allowed to choose the dress. I went with a pink pinstriped cotton jumper over a white blouse. Pink was my favorite color. Madee knew this but usually insisted on getting me itchy gray flannel dresses, or even worse, navy wool skirts and sweaters. The highlight of this trip, however, was the shoes. Madee wanted me to get the usual black patent leather Mary Janes; I chose brown leather Hush Puppies. In retrospect, I would have been better off with the Mary Janes. All the other girls in my class wore Mary Janes.

❧

When I visited my grandparents in Florida over Christmas vacation, Madee always took me to the Lilac Bush. On my first trip there, we found a parking spot right outside on Palmetto Park Boulevard and rushed inside to beat the rain. It always rained in Boca over Christmas vacation—always.

"Hello, I'm Helene Deitz, this is my granddaughter Rachel Levy, and we will be needing some help." This ritualistic introduction continually embarrassed me. Why should the whole store stop for us? The nice lady proceeded to help us with what we needed. I was happy with our selections: a cowgirl jumper and white ruffled blouse, a gray flannel dress with a white collar and red embroidered flowers, a bright green raincoat, and a turquoise sweat suit with pleated sleeves and little hearts on the chest and bottom side.

Then Madee told me the exciting news. Everything from the Lilac Bush would have my name embroidered on it. I was ecstatic. All I could think about was *Laverne & Shirley*. Would I be as cool as Laverne De Fazio with those fancy *L*s on her sweaters? To this day, some of my friends still call me Laverne, since many return visits to the Lilac Bush provided me with an ample "Rachel" wardrobe. Leave it to Madee to figure out that I would hand down those clothes to a family friend whose daughter's name was Rachel. As usual, Madee did not miss a beat.

ℭℜ

I felt like one of the girls. It was the Monday before Thanksgiving. I was in the fifth grade, and my mother allowed me to take the day off from school for a special trip to New York with her, Aunt Jo, and Madee. I carried one of my mother's old pocketbooks proudly as I secured a seat next to Mommy on the train. I listened to their conversations throughout the trip, picking up bits and pieces where I cared to.

We went to Saks Fifth Avenue, where Madee and I spent some quality time in the dressing room together. The goal of this trip was to purchase summer clothes, or cruise wear as they called it, for me to take down to Florida for the annual visit. I was growing like a weed, and last summer's clothes were not an option. I wanted the green-and-white vertical-striped pants, but Madee would not allow it. "They make you look too long and skinny." Although I hated to admit it, she was right. I ended up with two pink and red shorts and tops and white clam diggers, otherwise known as pedal pushers.

CR

Every summer, I went away to an all-girls camp in Maine, where we wore uniforms—blue shorts and white shirts. This meant very few summer-clothing shopping trips with Madee. Once I returned home from camp, however,

Madee was in full force for back-to-school shopping. One day, we checked out a trendy preteen store called Denim & Lace in one of the Philadelphia suburbs. The drop-waist sailor dresses were in style that year, and I couldn't wait to get one. Madee hesitatingly agreed to my request, but only if I got the one in red plaid wool. She could spot a trend from a mile away.

We ended up at Saks on City Line Avenue in Philadelphia later that day. After her usual introduction to the saleslady, Madee picked out a beautiful navy velvet dress with a white lace collar and navy satin sash. She told me to stand up straight as I tried it on, and that made all the difference. This was the dress for my brother's bar mitzvah. We both adored our selection. The best part was the white tights with purple, pink and blue flowers that I could wear with it. Since the bar mitzvah was in November, I needed a jacket as well. Madee's find—an emerald green fake-fur coat. I only wish that I had that jacket in my size today.

What I remember most about the bar mitzvah dress day is the lunch we had at Saks. Surrounded by tea sandwiches and mini pastries and feeling a bit like my favorite storybook character, Eloise, at the Plaza, I could not contain my smile from ear to ear. I was eleven years old and finally over my fear of this awesome figure in my life. I adored her. I loved to tell her about what was on my mind—the latest news from school, updates on my friends, even dreams about what I wanted to be when I grew up. As a shy young girl, these were things that I rarely discussed with anyone. Madee proceeded to tell me stories about what life was like for her growing up and for her daughters. I loved to imagine my mother as a little girl. I remember thinking that she sounded like a lot of fun—like someone whom I would want to have as my friend.

CR

One of the last major shopping experiences of my childhood was for my own bat mitzvah dress. When I was growing up in the Madonna and Cindy Lauper world of the 1980s, girls wore rhinestones on their dresses, or even worse, splattered paint. Madee would have nothing of the sort.

We purchased my bright red flowered corduroy dress at Laura Ashley. The white lace stockings and red velvet headband with a bow were also found at the preppy English store. My oldest friend, Julie, joined us on that day. She was bored out of her mind sitting in the dressing room as Madee searched through the racks for the dress that I would wear on the day that I became a woman—or so my religion told me. My mother always said that I was probably the only bat mitzvah girl who bought her dress at Laura Ashley. She was probably right.

CR

My first clue that Madee was becoming a little forgetful was on a typical shopping trip to Princeton. She wanted to see what was new at Jaeger (one of her signature stores), and I came along for the ride. We circled and circled around Palmer Square, the busy downtown area of the old college town. Madee could not figure out what had happened to her old reliable store.

I finally got out of the car and discovered the problem. Jaeger was where it had always been. However, they were filming the movie *I.Q.* with Walter Matthau in town, and the Jaeger sign had been replaced by a 1950s hardware-store sign. The rest of the building looked the same. I explained this to Madee, and we laughed together. I blamed the long search for Jaeger on the movie, but the real source of it was the beginning of Madee's dementia, which would last for years and years until she could shop no more.

# CHAPTER 2

MY MOTHER AND I were waiting patiently in a ski store out in Park City, Utah, while my brother and my father were figuring out what ski equipment to rent for the week. We headed over to the clothing area of the store, where we couldn't help but overhear a loud heavyset woman with a strong Chicago accent. She held a T-shirt up to the salesclerk that read, "My parents schlepped all the way to Park City, Utah and all I got was this lousy T-shirt." Waving the shirt in front of the saleslady, she said, "I'd love to get this shirt for my son Tommy, but what does *schlep* mean?" My mother's electric smile broke out on her face, and I could see her trying to contain her always-contagious laughter. We knew that *schlep* meant—well, it means to schlep—to drag yourself or something somewhere, and it was sort of a pain. We couldn't exactly help this woman out, but we laughed all the way home from the store. I loved to see my mother's smile. Everyone did.

ℂℝ

We were all very excited for my oldest cousin's wedding. I was seventeen, and the whole family was headed to England to see him marry his fantastic bride who had grown up in the English countryside. Shopping for weddings or any festive occasion was always a real treat for us. The catch here was that all the girls (as we referred to ourselves) had to wear hats to the wedding. That is what the English do, and when in Rome . . .

Aunt Jo, the mother of the groom, had done her research. She found out about a hat designer named Suzanne who made the headpieces for the then-up-and-coming wedding dress designer Vera Wang. I accompanied Aunt Jo into New York City that day. She needed a hat, and I needed a dress. The hat store was a tiny hole in the wall on Madison Avenue filled with proper-looking hats of all shapes and sizes. It was as if we had stepped into Queen Elizabeth's closet. Aunt Jo chose a big black straw hat with a sturdy brim and hand-sewn green, pink, and red flowers on it. She thought twice about showing up in another country as the mother of the groom with the black hat, but we agreed that it looked fabulous. She had to get it.

The hat lady, as we called her, rang up the price and said it out loud. To this day, that was the only time those numbers were uttered in public. We were not ones for sticker shock, but we (especially the seventeen-year-old me who was used to casual clothing prices from the Gap) could not believe our ears. This was her son's wedding, and Aunt Jo wanted the hat. She told me that the two of us would be the only ones to ever know its cost. Not even her husband, Uncle Dick, would find out. Aunt Jo paid all the bills. Besides, Uncle Dick would not care—he was not that way. I cannot, for the life of me, remember the price of that hat. I blocked it out so long ago because I was too scared to ever mention it again.

After the hat incident, Aunt Jo took me to Saks to find the perfect outfit for the "younger American cousin." Just like Madee, minus the silver hair and aging-face lines, Aunt Jo introduced herself to the saleswoman. "I am Joanne Hochman. This is my niece Rachel Levy, and she needs an outfit for my son's wedding in England." Now that the woman knew our life history, we could shop. I ended up with a knee-length red pleated chiffon skirt and blue-yellow-and-red plaid blazer with rhinestones on the shoulders. I kind of hated it, but Aunt Jo said it was perfect, so that was what I wore. She insisted I get the blue lace gloves and Ali McGraw—style hat with a yellow flower on it. The accessories, I liked.

☙

I always assumed that one of them would be with me to get my prom dress, but it didn't exactly turn out that way. I was in Boston, visiting a camp friend, and we went browsing along the trendy Newbury Street. Betsey Johnson was a popular designer for girls my age at the time. I insisted that we go in the store because Madee, Aunt Jo, and my mother had once bought me a dress there, for another cousin's wedding, without me. This happened a lot. All they ever needed was my size. They knew what I liked better than I did.

There, we found a short black taffeta dress with spaghetti straps and light pink roses sewn onto it. I loved it, but did not know what to do without my family there. This was before the days of cell phones. I asked the woman behind the counter if I could use her phone. Since it was a long-distance call, I took out the family emergency calling card and phoned my mother to ask her opinion. I described it to her in detail, and she thought it was a great idea. "Buy it," she said. The idea of making a purchase without the in-person approval of one of them was so foreign to me. I guess I was growing up. When Madee came to see me off before the prom, she gave me kudos for shopping on my own, just as she told my mother that the dress was too short.

CR

Back-to-school shopping before my freshman year in college was a big deal (in my mind at least). I was working at a day camp during the summer before I went away to school. Madee, Aunt Jo, and my mother took the liberty of preparing me for the collegiate world by themselves while I coached dodge ball in the summer heat. They came home from New York with a great pair of tan lace-up suede shoe boots that had brightly-colored embroidered flowers on them. I ended up wearing the boots through all four cold winters at school.

Of course, they couldn't just buy me the boots and have that be the end of it. While in the "lower-end" shoe department at Bergdorf Goodman that day, they came across a girl who looked about my age and was buying the same pair of boots. They explained their situation to her and asked if she thought I would like them too. During the course of their conversation, they discovered that she and I were both going to be freshmen at Penn in the fall. There was no phone number exchange. After all, this Bergdorf girl could have been a lunatic! When Mommy came home that day, she told me to look for the cute girl with my boots. "I am sure that in a class of two thousand students," I told her, "I will easily find this girl."

A couple of months into my first semester, I was drifting off a bit in my history of the 1960s class (which my mother did not think was a history class at all, but rather, a current, or at least recent, events class.) My head felt heavy as it fell toward the ground. I saw my flowered boots in front of me. The boot girl, as we called her, was in this freshman seminar class. I did not have the nerve to remind her of the infamous meeting. The freshman classroom was not a good place to mention Bergdorf Goodman. I made sure not to wear the boots to that class all semester.

# CHAPTER 3

AFTER CONVINCING MY parents that it was safe for me to live off-campus in West Philadelphia, I then explained how I would need to buy furniture for my room in the house. The university would no longer supply me with a bed, desk, and dresser. My mother agreed to come down and check out the old row house that I had been raving about and already signed the lease on. She would then help me pick out the furniture. After taking Mommy on a full tour of the house, including the slanted floors, the triple locks on the doors, and the basement (which had a very minor rat problem), I asked her what she thought. The woman, who was famous for handing out compliments as if they were going out of style, could not think of one good thing to say—she cried.

Her spirits lifted, though, as we entered the used-furniture store down the street. Mommy introduced herself to the man at the store. "My daughter is a student at Penn, and we need to furnish her room. We really want to make it look cute." He had a live one. We picked out a semi-fake wooden desk, a chair, two dressers, and a decent box spring and mattress. For the first time in my life, I had a full bed. We had already purchased the comforter from Bed Bath & Beyond—a Laura Ashley quilt with purple and yellow flowers. As my mother said, it took longer for me to pick the quilt than it did to pick the college. The twin from the dorm just wouldn't do. Mommy and I did not discuss my need for a larger bed. She knew how it worked these days when you had a real college boyfriend.

ᏨᏒ

"It looks like a slip." That was Mommy's reaction to my first real sophisticated dress. "That's why they call it a slip dress," I tried to explain to her outside of the dressing room at Knit Wit in Philadelphia. "I don't know where you are going in that," countered my mother. That was one of her classic lines. It has stuck in my head to this day. Even if I love something, I will ask myself where I think I am going in it. If I can't come up with an answer, I can't get it.

On this day, however, I was fully prepared for that remark and gave her one reason from the list in my head.

I told her I had a million (meaning two) fraternity and sorority parties to go to. "All right, you can get it, but we'll show it to Aunt Jo first just, to make sure." *Yes!* I thought. Aunt Jo would love it. She was a bit more hip than my mother, and I wasn't her daughter, so what did she care if I looked like a complete slut? We stopped at Aunt Jo's house on the way home. "Fabulous," she said in her typical excited voice. That was that. Whatever my mother's sister said was gospel. The Knit Wit slip dress was a keeper.

CR

On a typical summer day spent strolling around the town of Princeton, my mother took me to the new Banana Republic. She asked me if I needed anything special for my up-and-coming senior year in college. "No," I shrugged, feeling sorry for myself after being dumped by my college boyfriend (which turned out to be the best thing for me). "Well let's just look anyway," she said. That was pure Becky Levy—always looking on the bright side of things.

We spent a long time in the Banana (as my friends and I called it). Mommy convinced me that I would need the black flowy pants and peasant top for dinners, parties, or just hanging out with friends. She insisted on the two wool miniskirts and ribbed turtlenecks, as well as the suede jacket. For once, I felt like asking her where she thought I was going in that. I almost broke out in tears sitting next to her on the little changing-room bench.

"This year is going to suck. All my friends have boyfriends, and I am going to be left at home with nothing to do." My mother would not stand for talk like this. "Buck up, Rach," as she often said. "You are a beautiful, intelligent, wonderful person with so much going for you, and if you don't stop sulking, you will wake up one day to discover that you let the best years of your life pass you by." That was Mommy. She wouldn't let you or anyone around you feel sorry for yourself. She gave me confidence that afternoon as she did every day of my life. Right there in the Banana changing room, I started to feel a little better about myself. I had places to go and clothes to wear.

CR

I tried to explain to my mother that I needed a real skirt suit to wear to job interviews. I was a senior in college, and many of the companies that I was interested in working for would be coming to campus. Mommy thought that it would be fine for me to "look nice in a lovely skirt and sweater." That was not happening. After leaving the parents' weekend football game early, the two of us went to the Banana Republic in downtown Philadelphia.

I wanted something classic—a black knee-length skirt and jacket—something that wouldn't make me stand out. The interviewer should remember me for my accomplishments and experiences, not for my outfit. Mommy tried to explain to me that I would look like a frumpy old lady in such a conservative suit. She somehow convinced me to get a brown tweed jacket and matching short skirt with orange stripes. She insisted that I wear them with brown tights and brown high-heeled Mary Janes, which we bought later that day.

On one hand, I thought this was crazy, but at the same time, I always trusted my mother. She came from good stock and wasn't wrong about many things. That day at the Philadelphia Banana, she also reminded me that it was okay for me not to look like or be like everyone else. This was a big rule of thumb in my family. I was Rachel Levy, and there was no one else like me. Who knows if I got that first job in publishing after college because of me or because of my suit. Either way, I was happy with the outcome.

CR

The first time I ever wore any makeup for real was on Aunt Jo's back deck at her house in Yardley, Pennsylvania. She gave me a mini makeover and tried to explain to me how to do it myself. She then instructed me to go to Henri Bendel's in New York City (I was living there while working after college) all by myself and ask for Mickey. Mickey would hook me up with the right products, and I would be magically transformed into a real professional young woman.

Aunt Jo was a bit of a revolutionary in the makeup department as far as the rest of my family was concerned. Madee was still wearing the same rouge she had bought in 1940, and my mother would not go anywhere without her Estée Lauder coral lipstick. That color is forever embedded in my memory, as I washed it off my cheek every night following her welcome-home-from-school kisses. After spending some time with Mickey at the Trish McEvoy counter in Bendel's, I called my mother from the phone in the store. (Over the years, I have used many store phones to check in with my committee of shoppers.) The only reason my mother thought that the new makeup idea was a good one was because it was Aunt Jo's. A few weeks later, I met Mommy at Bendel's, where Mickey proceeded to make her over. It was out with the old coral lipstick and in with the new softer tones of roses and browns.

# CHAPTER 4

I THOUGHT THAT someone from the family would come into New York City to help me pick out furniture for my first apartment that was just mine—no roommates this time. The plans changed, however, when, in March of 1998, my mother's ophthalmologist (who happened to be her cousin) found a malignant tumor in her eye. She was diagnosed with ocular melanoma—a rare form of the skin cancer that affects the eye. She had a radioactive plaque put on the eye to shrink the size of the tumor. Her prognosis was good. The eye tumor was dead, and chances were very low that any tumors would come back.

While my mother sat in Wills Eye Hospital in Philadelphia for several days with radiation pumping into her eye, I tried to pick out furniture for my apartment. I was forbidden to see her in the hospital. No person of childbearing age could come visit as the massive amounts of radiation could affect the fertility of that person. I pleaded with my mother for a visit, but she wouldn't allow it. "Rach, I am absolutely fine. I am doing my job here, and I want you to do your job and decorate your new place. I'll come to New York when I am better, and I can't wait to see it."

Madee and Aunt Jo spent the next several days at Wills Eye along with my father, grandfather, and other family members and friends. My then-boyfriend, Neil, accompanied me on my trip to Pottery Barn. Neil was amazed at the speed with which I furnished an entire apartment. I could hear Madee's, Aunt Jo's, and Mommy's voices in my head. "It's not that difficult to furnish one tiny apartment." Neil looked on as I selected a couch, table and chairs, a comfy chair, as well as plates, glasses, and silverware. He had never seen my shopping skills in action. I could see that he was both impressed and scared. I thanked him for coming and holding my hand that day. I knew he was a keeper.

Neil loved me for me. He loved the idiosyncrasies. He loved that I could be so independent. He loved my friends and my family and the relationships that I already had with them. That was important. Other men may have felt threatened by those already established bonds, but not Neil. He knew they were a big part of my life, and he jumped right in. It was only later, when times got tough, that I would truly come to know how much I could and would depend on him. "Salt of the earth," that was how a friend described Neil, and he could not have been more right. They didn't come any better. The best values, the best sense of humor, and the best smile.

☙

I never really understood the concept of a wedding registry until I had to do it myself. It seemed strange to pick out gifts that other people would buy for me. Only a week after I got engaged to Neil in the spring of 1999, Aunt Jo and my mother headed to New York to help me with our registry. The plan was that I would meet them at the store during my lunch break from work. We would pick out what we liked, and I'd take Neil back over the weekend to actually register.

Mommy called me at work from her cell phone. "We already went to Bloomingdale's, and they were most unhelpful there. Aunt Jo's friend, Louise, told us about this wonderful store called Michael C. Fina. It's fabulous. Meet us there as soon as you can." I tied up my loose ends at work and told my boss that I had a very long lunch meeting to attend. Upon entering the store on the corner of Forty-fifth Street and Fifth Avenue, I saw the two sisters standing with a long list in their hands and huge grins on their faces. They had actually gone through the entire store with the saleswoman and picked out our registry.

"I can't believe you picked out everything. Isn't this stuff for Neil and me?" I asked. They played good defense. "You can change anything you want or do a whole new registry. We just wanted to help." Okay, I would go around the store with them and pick what I wanted. After about a half hour of explanations on china patterns, crystals, and stainless silver, I realized that Aunt Jo and Mommy were the experts in this field. I knew magazine publishing—they knew registering. They picked out the perfect registry, and I did not change a thing. I took Neil back to Michael C. Fina that weekend. He had the same initial reaction as I did. It took him five minutes, however, to realize that registering was not his forte. He made one addition—beer steins. That's all he wanted.

⚜

My mother called me the night before I was going to meet her and her sister to shop for my wedding dress. She left two instructions on my answering machine. "Eat a good breakfast and look like a person." I was known for skipping breakfast and feeling faint later in the day. Mommy knew that I needed my energy for the big day. "Look like a person" was Mommy's way of telling me to not wear jeans—my weekend uniform. She always wanted me to look nice when we went shopping. I never understood this. The point of shopping was to replace your current clothes.

I woke up early on that Saturday morning. After a big bowl of cereal, I got dressed in black pants, a cashmere sweater set, and even put on the Hermès scarf that my mother had bought me when she was in Paris. I felt like an old lady—"a person," according to Mommy's standards. I walked through the park and met Aunt Jo and my mother inside Vera Wang, the famous bridal boutique. They walked down the winding stairway with Renee, the woman who would be helping us, as if they had been waiting for this moment all my life. "You look nice," they echoed each other and then gave me a big hug and a kiss.

As we walked back up the stairs to check out the dresses, Mommy held my hand and told me that she always thought Madee would help me pick out my wedding dress. I always loved the feel of Mommy's small well-manicured hand in mine. Madee could not make it to New York. Her dementia was accelerating, and she was on the verge of breaking a hip.

Mommy told Renee that she pictured me in a long-sleeved gown. Aunt Jo and Mommy wore the same long-sleeved gown to their weddings some thirty years prior. Renee explained how Vera (no last name—they were tight) liked to dress the young brides in sleeveless or strapless gowns—long sleeves were for matrons, not brides.

Renee showed us a whole rack of beautiful gowns. I immediately chose a strapless off-white duchess satin gown with Swarovski crystals, a scalloped top, full skirt, and blue satin bow at the waist. Aunt Jo and Mommy flinched at that one, but I tried it on, nonetheless. I walked out of the dressing room in it. We all knew that this was the one. They told me I looked gorgeous—like Grace Kelly, said Mommy (generous with the compliments, as usual). Then she asked Aunt Jo if she remembered when I was such an ugly baby. Renee laughed. Honesty was still the key in our family. I proceeded to try on a slew of other dresses, including one that Aunt Jo said made me look like a lampshade. The Grace Kelly one was the keeper. We picked out a colorful crystal tiara to wear in my hair, along with a floor-length tulle veil trimmed in satin, and decided on which antique jewelry from Madee's collection would look right with the dress.

Throughout that morning, we became friendly with the woman and her friends and her sister who were picking out her wedding dress next to us. Once they had decided on the dress, the older sister announced that she would be buying the gown for her younger sister. Their mother had died years ago, and this was her gift. The girls cried as we looked on and smiled. Renee then told me how lucky I was that my mother was getting me such a beautiful dress. I knew that I was lucky, but not to have the dress. I was lucky to have Mommy and Aunt Jo there with me.

CR

Aunt Jo called me at work one day from Bergdorf Goodman. She had come to the city to do a preliminary look for a dress that Mommy would wear to my wedding. Mommy certainly could not have selected a dress without our help. "Can you meet me on the dressy floor"—as she called it—"now?" It was another long-lunch day for me. The summer before my wedding was one of the busiest times at my office. My boss had just left, we were budgeting for the next year, and I was working on the launch of a new magazine. Aunt Jo and my mother were aware of the situation, so they ran the show and called me when needed. My coworkers could always tell when I received a call from Mommy or Aunt Jo. The walls were thin, and I had a very loud voice. "It sounds like you'll have red roses in your bouquet," a colleague of mine announced as I walked into a meeting straight off a call with Mommy.

I met Aunt Jo at Bergdorf Goodman, and she showed me an adorable knee-length dark purple dress with a flounce and black lace and beading around the collar. We both agreed that this was a good selection for Mommy, along with a few other similar styles. We knew that Mommy did not want to look like a typical mother of the bride in a cream jacket and skirt. Aunt Jo brought Mommy into the city the next week to have her try on the preselected choices. Mommy called me from the dressing room. I had some people in my office, but caller ID told me that I had to pick it up. "I am standing here in the dress that I am wearing to your wedding. Can you come over and check it out?"

My curiosity got the best of me. In the sticky July city heat, I walked up the seven blocks from the Time-Life Building to the good old Bergdorf Goodman dressy floor. My mother was standing there in a long-sleeved, off-the-shoulder, floor-length pale green Mary McFadden gown with hand-sewn coral, pearls, crystals, and gold beads. She looked like a Victorian doll. It was the most gorgeous thing I had ever seen. Mommy looked fabulous even though it was not her typical style. My mother always wore simple tea-length dresses that swished around the room while she danced the waltz with my father or the Charleston with my grandfather.

This creation was very sophisticated. Aunt Jo told me that my mother had picked it out all by herself. I was so proud of my mother (who always relied on her mother, sister, or daughter for advice). Little Becky Levy was growing up. I know that all brides are the prettiest girls at the wedding. I say this in all honesty and without any jealousy whatsoever. On the night of my wedding, my mother was the prettiest one in the room, and I could not have been happier.

CR

Aunt Jo used to say that every time I had a boyfriend, she would polish the silver, preparing for the engagement party that she would have for me one day. The time had finally arrived. She and my Aunt Linda were planning an evening party for us, and ten of my mother's closest friends were having a bridal shower for me. (Not to mention the party being given by one of my grandmother's friends.) The number of events was a testament to the kind of person that my mother was. Everybody loved her.

I needed clothes to wear to these various soirees. Aunt Jo and my mother suggested that I come back home for this shopping event. We'd go to Angel Heart, a boutique in Newtown, Pennsylvania, that had very unique items. I brought my friend, Penny, out from the city that weekend. She came along on the shopping excursion. The four of us basically took over the store that afternoon. Penny was a good sport to sit through all of it.

There was no modesty in my family. We often did not require a changing room in a small store such as Angel Heart. We just stripped down right in front of everyone—it was easier than going back and forth into the tiny room. We did have to be careful, however, that the occasional UPS man or lingering husband did not catch a glimpse. On that day, the whole store was my changing room. We were on a mission and did not have time to be shy.

Aunt Jo convinced my mother to get me a pink sweater set with purple sewn-on flowers and a shiny purple silk skirt with slits on it for the engagement party. She insisted that I looked like Gwyneth Paltrow in it. (Aunt Jo had a tendency to exaggerate how great you really looked.) To me it was more the preppy-girl-posing-as-a-flapper look. I also ended up with a see-through gray peasant blouse with little blue daisies and a gray wool pencil skirt with blue trim to wear to the daytime shower. My mother never liked that choice. We managed to find a black velvet tea-length skirt and gray fitted chenille sweater with a velvet collar and jeweled buttons. This was the rehearsal dinner ensemble. Or, as Mommy said, "what you'll wear the night before you walk down the aisle."

While we were at Angel Heart, my mother managed to keep Penny occupied as Aunt Jo and I selected evening bags for my bridesmaids as gifts for their participation in the wedding. My mother saw Penny looking at a pair of earrings in the store and immediately bought them for her. "You were a good sport, Penny. You deserve them," said Mommy. All my friends loved my mother. She always expressed interest in what they were doing and was most caring and giving to them. She was their Auntie Mame. Penny still wears those earrings, and we laugh about the sacrifice that she made for me that day.

CR

Although Madee was getting older and more forgetful, she often looked more put together and beautiful than most young women. My grandfather, Padee, always made sure that she had on earrings and lipstick before she left the house. Aunt Jo and my mother took her to an old boutique in Trenton, New Jersey, called Stacy to find a dress for my wedding. This was the place to shop when Madee was a younger woman, and they still had pretty things for her.

It was difficult to pick out a dress for Madee as she had become extremely thin, and the hump on her upper back grew larger as her osteoporosis worsened. To an outsider, she looked like an old lady. To me, she looked like my elegant Madee. They decided on a simple navy blue knee-length silk dress with a matching jacket. This shopping trip was not as lighthearted as most of the other ones. It was a struggle to get Madee in and out of the dress and to keep reminding her why they were shopping at all.

Despite breaking her hip ten days before my wedding, Madee came to the event in the dress from Stacy. She could not walk down the aisle with my grandfather as we had originally planned, but she sat in the front row looking on lovingly. By that point, Madee usually did not know where she was. On the evening of my wedding, however, she told my grandfather how "lovely it was to be at Rachel's wedding." She was buried in that blue dress—her last purchase—just one year later.

CR

On a hot August day in Washington, D.C., I stood by my grandfather's side at the gift shop of the Smithsonian museum. Our family was in the capital city for my cousin's wedding. The young men in the family were off on a prenuptial golf outing while my mother and I spent the afternoon shopping around town with Padee. I was thrilled that Padee made it down for the weekend. Madee had passed away only two months prior. My mother had arranged for a cabdriver to take us around the city. She would not risk her father's health in the sultry heat.

After seeing many of the wonders at the Smithsonian Institute, we ended up where we always did—in the gift shop. Padee picked out an intricate pair of silver-and-turquoise earrings for me, as well as a modern plastic red watch for Mommy. He then announced that we had to pick something out for Madee to bring to her back home. At age ninety-two, my grandfather had all his marbles. In fact, he had proven himself and beat me at Jeopardy countless times. Padee was simply so used to always getting a present for Madee—"the kid," as he called her. I took his strong freckled tan hand in mine and gave it a tight squeeze. My mother leaned in and planted a kiss on his bald head. He nodded at us as if to say, "I know—force of habit." Padee passed away the following summer.

# CHAPTER 5

I WAS SLIGHTLY nervous for my parents' visit out to Ann Arbor in the fall of 2001. Neil and I were in business school at the University of Michigan. Just one month after we had moved out there, we got the news that my mother's ocular melanoma had metastasized to her liver. This was not good. However, Mommy was under the best care possible at Jefferson University Hospital right in Philadelphia, and she had a phenomenal attitude. She was undergoing experimental treatments that sought to cut off the blood supply to the bad cells in the liver so that the cancerous cells would die. I wanted to come home when we got the initial news. My mother, being my mother, insisted that I stay in school and focus on my graduate studies and my life with Neil. "Don't ever use me as a crutch," she said.

We met my parents at their hotel for breakfast the morning they arrived in Ann Arbor, and Mommy looked terrific—never better. She was decked out in a brightly colored sweater set, Hermès scarf, and big hoop earrings. I remember laughing at her as I explained that she did not exactly blend in the Midwest college town.

After giving them a tour of the campus, it was off to the Ann Arbor mall. (Not the greatest place on earth, but it would have to do.) Neil went home to watch the football game on television and avoid an entire afternoon outing of shopping. My mother sat in the dressing room in J.Crew while my father browsed through the store and I tried on jeans, sweaters, and corduroys. Mommy was practical with our selections. "You certainly don't need dressy clothes out here." My favorite purchase from that day was a charcoal gray wool sweater coat. I wore it on the days when Mommy would have a treatment. For some reason, I thought it would bring good luck.

This shopping excursion felt different. She wanted to buy me everything. "Just get them in both colors," she kept saying. Daddy smiled and agreed as usual. I was thankful, as always, and tried not to think too much about why we left the mall with so many items. I held Mommy's tiny hand all the way back to the car in the parking lot on that damp Michigan day.

☙

Embolizations were what the doctors called my mother's monthly treatments, and they were going well. She had very few side effects, and the tumors were shrinking. We could not have been more pleased. Mommy received a different present from Aunt Jo every month before each treatment. This required Aunt Jo to make extra special shopping trips all over town, and she outdid herself every time. Mommy was the best-dressed and accessorized patient on the fifth floor of Jefferson University Hospital.

I did some shopping of my own to keep Mommy smiling throughout her treatments. I sent cards every month from Ann Arbor. I found myself laughing out loud in the local Hallmark store. Over time, I got to know the woman that worked behind the cash register. She was happy to see me come back to the store each month for another card. Each card meant a new treatment, and a new month of hope. Mommy saved every one of those cards. They filled up her kitchen bulletin board in a colorful paper mosaic.

While away at school, I always knew that Mommy's days were good. Aunt Jo kept her on the go. The two of them, now more than ever, headed to the little boutiques that they loved in Newtown and Princeton. To say they were regulars was an understatement. They no longer needed an excuse to go shopping. Mommy did not wait to be invited to a party to buy an outfit. She bought them simply to have—to know that she might have the chance to wear them in the future. An uncertain future that somehow became brighter with every trip to the store.

CR

Aunt Jo took Mommy up to the gourmet food store in New Hope to select holiday gifts for her doctors. The dynamic duo picked out cheeses, fruits, pâtés, crackers, candies, dishes, and more. When Drs. Sato and Eschelman received the baskets, they were amazed, but in some ways, not surprised. They adored Mommy for all the smiles she gave them, for her upbeat attitude, for never complaining, and for allowing them to learn more in their research studies. Mommy was one of their star patients for all these reasons and more.

After taking care of the doctors, she headed over to her dear friend Roz's house. Roz's husband was in the watch business. On this day, Mommy shopped from one of the watch catalogs—something she rarely did, as she loved selecting the items in person. But this year, she was making things easy on herself. Mommy picked out fourteen watches—one for every nurse, secretary, and lab technician. I went down to the hospital on my Christmas break for Mommy's embolization, along with my father and Aunt Jo, who both never missed a treatment. Mommy was just like Santa Claus—handing out gifts to everyone as they wheeled her along the hospital floor in the gurney. Mommy, the sick patient, lifted the spirits of the healthy hospital staff.

CR

While Mommy may have missed out on helping me decorate my first apartment, she would surely be there to select the furniture for our first house. She and Aunt Jo were the ones who actually found our first house when they heard that it was on the market through friends. Neil and I would be graduating from business school and moving to our home in Yardley—right near my family. Aunt Jo and Mommy went to the Thomasville Furniture Store in town to do a walk-through on their selection before we came home for the actual purchasing day.

On furniture-selection day, my mother came fully equipped to the store with measurements and pictures of each room in the house. Once again, Neil was amazed at the speed and decisiveness in our shopping that day. We decided on an oak kitchen table and chairs with forest green legs (yes, green) and a matching hutch. Neil agreed to the unconventional colors, but he had some issues when we starting picking out the fabrics for the living room furniture. A lot of the wooden pieces for the living room were antiques from my grandparents' house. They were beautiful and sentimental. I had my heart set on a toile print for the couch. Neil felt strongly that nowhere in his house would there be "people or flowers on the fabric." Aunt Jo saw his point, so I conceded. (Neil always knew how to get to me: just go through the boss—Aunt Jo.) We selected plaid, plain, and dotted fabrics in raspberries, yellows, and greens, along with wooden end tables and stools.

We wanted to pick out a couch for the den that day, but my mother was losing energy. She became a little overwhelmed and tired. As she sat down on one of the sample sofas in the store, Aunt Jo shot me a look, and I knew that this was too much for Mommy. She had been undergoing her treatments for a year and a half by this point.

Mommy put on a good show over the phone or on our short visits every few months. Now that I was seeing her day to day, I could tell that she wasn't her old self. We forged through that day, however, and twelve weeks later, my mother arrived at the new house to greet the Thomasville deliverymen, who arrived promptly with the new furniture.

CR

Our baby was due just four months from the day we closed the sale of the house. I was getting along with some of my "fat clothes" as my stomach expanded, but they could take me only so far. Mommy insisted that we go check out A Pea in the Pod, the upscale maternity store. Aunt Jo, Mommy, and I headed down to the King of Prussia Mall to see the latest mother-to-be fashions. As we searched through the racks, Mommy recounted how Madee had taken her maternity-clothes-shopping way back when and bought her the "most beautiful" white linen dress. I gave her a smile and a quick peck on the cheek. "Thank you for everything," I said. "It's my pleasure," was always her answer.

Aunt Jo took the lead, selecting cute capri pants, a jeans jacket, a few sweater sets, a Lilly Pulitzer bathing suit, a tie-dyed T-shirt with ruffled sleeves, and several long-sleeved T-shirts. I wanted to get a pair of Seven maternity jeans—the hot new item in maternity wear. Aunt Jo and Mommy told me that they made my "rear end look big." They were right as usual, and I was always happy to have their honest opinions.

CR

The baby was due in less than two months so Aunt Jo, Mommy, and I headed down to Philadelphia to pick out the layette. I did not know much about this process, but I was excited to finally be looking at things for the new baby—or the Doctor, as we called it. We did not know the gender of the baby, but Neil and I were pretty sure that we would name it for my grandfather, who had died the previous summer. Padee's real name was Joseph, but he was an orthopedic surgeon, and everyone called him Doctor. One day, Neil said to me, "Whether we have a boy or a girl, we'll just name the baby Doctor." The nickname has stuck with the child until this day.

We knew Amethyst, the saleswoman at the Children's Boutique very well. Every month, when my mother came down to Philadelphia for her treatments, my father, Aunt Jo, and I would stroll up to the store to kill time and to pick out clothing for Aunt Jo's grandchildren who lived in

London. Today, it felt good to have Mommy with us. At first, Amethyst was a bit surprised to see my mother there. I think she had assumed, from all of our previous visits, that Aunt Jo was my mother and married to my father. How could she know that my actual mother was lying on a hospital bed ten blocks south under a local anesthetic while life-saving medicine was being injected into her liver?

Amethyst explained how we would select clothes for a boy and a girl. After the baby was born, we would call her with the big news, and she would send the proper items to our house. (In the Jewish tradition, it is bad luck to have any baby items in the home before the baby arrives.) We picked out onesies, blankets, nightgowns, hats, socks, dressy outfits, towels, and linens. My mother went nuts over the linens, insisting on yellow-and-white gingham with embroidered scenes of "The Cat and the Fiddle" all around. Aunt Jo purchased the matching quilt and diaper stacker for us.

Our favorite piece of the day was the white linen bassinette with yellow piping. Mommy adored it, and she told me how she would wrap a red ribbon on the side of it to ward off evil spirits—a superstition she learned from her friend Inez. The three of us left the store with big smiles on our faces, feeling satisfied with the shopping, and looking forward to a new baby in the family. We headed to the Rittenhouse Hotel for a delicious lunch. I knew how special it was to have my mother there along with Aunt Jo. It had been almost two years since the metastasized melanoma was discovered, and it looked like Mommy was in good shape to meet her first grandchild.

# CHAPTER 6

MY BROTHER, JONNY, became engaged in the late spring of 2003. The wedding would be the following February in Miami, where his fiancée, Jill, had grown up. My family was thrilled about the good news and so excited, for my mother's sake, to have another happy occasion waiting for us down the road. This time, Mommy was the mother of the groom. As she said, she would simply "buy a dress and show up." Jill had requested that Mommy wear black to the wedding, so off she went with her sister to find the black dress.

The dynamic duo headed to New York in the late summer of 2003 for some shopping and to see a Broadway show. I sat this one out as the baby was due a month later, and I did not feel up to venturing into the city. On that day, Aunt Jo and Mommy held hands while they sang and laughed along to *Avenue Q*, the new musical about recent college graduates trying to find their way in New York. It was the happy, puppet-show version of *Rent*. My mother loved musicals—especially the ones where she left the theater "singing in the aisles." I can still feel her smiling eyes on me as I gazed up at Sandy Duncan flying through the sky in *Peter Pan* when I was a young child. When Peter and Wendy asked the audience to clap if we believed in fairies, my mother's hands moved just as quickly as all of the children's. She believed in Tinkerbell and all good things.

Before the show, they made a stop at Bergdorf Goodman in search of the mother-of-the groom dress. Just a few weeks before their New York City day, Dr. Sato had informed my mother that the embolizations were not as successful as they had once been. After two years of the treatments, he recommended taking a break and starting a new drug called Thalidomide. Thalidomide was actually an old drug given to pregnant women in the 1960s to treat their nausea. The medicine was taken off the market years later when it was discovered to be the cause of severe birth defects. In recent clinical trials, however, it was thought that Thalidomide could systemically kill off cancer cells. It was worth a try.

Mommy was aware of the potential side effects—weight gain, constipation, extreme fatigue—and she experienced them all. She managed to keep her energy up that day at Bergdorf's. As she sat with her baby sister in the dressing room, Aunt Jo noticed Mommy's larger-than-usual stomach. Was it from the medicine or the tumors in the liver? Aunt Jo did not know. Mommy was becoming upset that she could no longer fit into her old dress size. Always thinking on her feet, Aunt Jo promptly headed out to the floor and found an elegant ruffled black velvet Valentino skirt and a black cashmere sweater with jeweled cuffs. Mommy would not be the typical mother of the groom in this ensemble, but no one expected that of her. Best of all, the skirt could expand with her stomach. The girls did not discuss that issue, but they knew it to be true.

ᘓ

The three of us spent the day together for Mommy's fifty-seventh birthday. Our dear friend Inez joined us on a trip down to Neiman Marcus at the King of Prussia Mall. We wandered around the shoe department in search of the right footwear for Mommy for the wedding—no luck. Next, it was off to the café at Neiman's.

I had not been with my mother on her birthday in almost fifteen years, as I was always away at school or working. This day, as so many of them were, was special. We laughed at lunch as I explained to them that the baby kept kicking whenever I pulled out a pretty dress from the racks at the store. For that reason, I was convinced it was a girl, and so was my mother. Inez treated us to lunch and arranged for a rich chocolate cake to be sent over with candles in honor of Mommy's big day. She made a wish—we all knew what for—and blew them out.

CR

About six weeks into the Thalidomide treatments, Mommy began to feel quite nauseous. She had assumed this was from the medicine. Aunt Jo knew better. For the first time in over two years of living with metastatic melanoma, Mommy was beginning to be symptomatic. I called Aunt Jo and confronted her on the issue—she would never lie to me. I was finally beginning to come to terms with my mother's mortality. Aunt Jo had known all along, but she continued to follow my mother's positive lead. She explained to me how, for my mother's sake, I must do the same.

Aunt Jo showed up at Mommy's doorstep on that nauseous morning and convinced her that she needed boots for her upcoming ski trip out to Utah with my father. I could not join them as our baby boy, Joseph Deitz Lesser (named for Padee), was only six weeks old. The sisters headed down to the shoe department in Nordstrom. Somewhere in between the lace-up shearlings and the high-heeled suede boots, Mommy had forgotten all about her upset stomach.

CR

By November of 2003, my father, brother, and the rest of the family had come to realize that the tumors in Mommy's liver could not be contained forever, and that her days were numbered. The doctors had explained this to us, but it still seemed surreal. Mommy walked around with the same bounce in her step and smile on her face as she did when she was well. Since the Thalidomide was not doing the trick, Mommy went back to the embolizations in a more aggressive format. She was returning from the hospital the week before Aunt Jo, Aunt Linda, and I were throwing a bridal shower for my brother's fiancée.

I got a babysitter so that Aunt Jo could take me to Newtown to find an outfit for the shower and the engagement party given by my mother's friends. Aunt Jo went ahead to Priorities for Her, the women's store in town. She selected a black Diane von Fürstenburg top with a low back and a leopard-print skirt. It sounded cheesy to me, but I trusted Aunt Jo, and it ended up looking great. For the evening party, she picked a short red-and-black wrap dress with a matching slip by the same designer. I fell in love with that one.

We went right next door to the Shoe Café and found adorable brown-and-tan pointy heels with a bow at the top to wear for the shower. I already had black shoes that would be perfect with the dress. I called Mommy several times that day from the store to give her the updates. She was resting at home, so I promptly brought the outfits over and gave her a fashion show right in the bedroom. She loved everything and loved that Aunt Jo could take me—never once did she feel sorry for herself at home. "You are lucky to have Aunt Jo," she said. I blew that comment off, not wanting to think about what she was really saying. I did know I was lucky.

☙

When Mommy was well rested enough from her treatment, Aunt Jo and I took her, along with baby Joey, into Newtown to find her own clothes for the pre-wedding events. The women helping us at Angel Heart that day could see that Mommy's abdomen was distended. They said nothing and simply brought her tops in bigger sizes. Mommy was starting not to look like herself. Besides the stomach, her skin looked jaundiced due to the slowdown of her liver's functions. People just assumed that she was tan.

Nina, the owner of Angel Heart, had become our friend through the years. She selected a large gray wool jacket with embroidered butterflies. Mommy was not thrilled with this oversized top at first. Aunt Jo and I quickly searched around the store for the right accessories. Once Mommy put on the large jeweled Erickson Beamon butterfly pin and dangling pink-and-green earrings, she felt better about herself. Another Becky Levy rule—there was no such thing as overaccessorizing.

❧

Aunt Jo was extremely self-sufficient when it came to shopping for herself. She had found a blue two-piece silk outfit for Jonny and Jill's wedding. I was the only one with nothing to wear. I was thrilled that Jill had asked me to be a bridesmaid, and even more thrilled to learn that I could select my own black dress for the wedding. By this time, I had been a bridesmaid six times, and six times, I wore the dress once and promptly gave it away.

At this point, my mother was feeling pretty tired. I wondered if she would make it to the wedding or if there would even be one just three months later. Finding a dress was not a priority for me, but Aunt Jo insisted that Mommy and I would have our day. "If I have to drive you up to the store and bring the dresses out to the car to show your mother, I will do so," said Aunt Jo. We set the date for the Friday before Thanksgiving to head to New York. I found a babysitter for Joey, and Aunt Jo made up an excuse as to why she couldn't come. She wanted Mommy and me to have this time together.

I picked Mommy up at her house, and we made the 8:13 a.m. train to New York. I told Mommy that I did not want to take the subway up to midtown as we usually did because it would be too crowded at that time of day. In truth, I knew Mommy could never handle the steps. The cab dropped us off right in front of Saks. After searching through the racks on the more reasonably priced floor, we headed to the fancy one. It was there that we found the sleeveless, tea-length black lace Monique Lhullier dress with a light pink satin ribbon around the waist. Mommy and I fell in love with it immediately, and it was the perfect fit.

We called Jill at her office from the dressing room to give her the rundown, and she enthusiastically approved. I thought that it was a pretty expensive purchase, but Mommy did not care. "It's special," as she often said, followed by "You have a good daddy," another one of the Becky Levy classics. We celebrated with lunch at the Saks café. She held my hand across the table and told me how pretty I would look on the day of the wedding. I tried to memorize the feel of her hand in mine as I secretly hoped that we would all make it to the wedding.

After Saks, we ventured on to Bergdorf's, where we each picked out hosiery for the wedding. As we crossed Fifth Avenue heading toward the Burberry store, I guarded Mommy from oncoming traffic and watched her closely just as she had done for me for so many years. She treated me to the pink Burberry "happy" scarf, as it said on the tag. This was not a Hanukkah or a birthday present. It was a just-because-I-love-you present. I picked out a wool baseball cap with the famous Burberry pattern for my mother. It fit like a glove on Mommy's tiny head, and she walked out of the store wearing it.

I have had many good days in my life thus far and hope to have many more. That day in New York goes down in my book as one of the best. I can still see each moment of it in my mind's eye. I have it on continual repeat mode just like the Baby Einstein videos that my son watches over and over again. I am forever grateful to have had that day.

ᏟᏗ

We were just two months away from the wedding, and Mommy was still not letting anything slow her down. I accompanied my father and Aunt Jo to one of Mommy's treatments on the day of my fourth wedding anniversary. My mother-in-law had driven down from New York to watch our three-month-old baby so that I could be at the hospital with Mommy.

Mommy was still in the procedure room, and her doctors had given us what was becoming the rather typical dismal report. We knew the score, and in many ways, so did Mommy. Still, she was determined to beat it and did not want to talk about the inevitable. I had just finished reading a book by a physician called *The Anatomy of Hope*. We were all convinced that there was a lot to be said for mind over matter, and Mommy was living proof. We all walked in to see her with big smiles on our faces.

After discussing how Mommy was right on course with her treatments, and how much we loved each other—something that we did every day—Mommy commented that my winter coat was not in such great shape. I laughed. Even under the power of heavy drugs, Mommy could spot a bad coat. Aunt Jo then remarked how Hedy Shepard, one of their favorite stores in Princeton, had just gotten in some cute coats. With that, they forced me out in the hallway. I speed-dialed the store from my mother's cell phone to hear about the latest selection.

There was Mommy shopping from her hospital bed. This made her feel good, as the experimental medicines tried to do their job and attach to the ever-growing cancerous cells in her abdomen. The next week, the three of us went over to Hedy's and purchased a new coat. Another day of shopping together, which made us all smile a lot.

# CHAPTER 7

WE ALL WENT away for New Year's Day 2004. My mother and my father ventured out west for a quick ski trip in Park City, Utah. Mommy had given up skiing long ago. She never liked the sport, but she enthusiastically joined us on the family ski trip every year. "I like everything that goes with it," Mommy would say. Day after day, she would patiently wait for us in the lodge, giving us updates of the latest goings-on from the cafeteria. This year, Mommy agreed to give Daddy his one last chance to ski before she forced him into early retirement. Daddy agreed to stay in the over-the-top Stein Eriksen Lodge in the middle of the mountain. Mommy had always wanted to stay there.

Neil and I were spending our first time apart from our four-month-old son. We left Joey with my in-laws and headed up to the Berkshires for the long weekend. I spent most of that trip in tears. Not because I missed my son (which I did, but I knew he was in good hands, and I felt that it was important for Neil and me to have our alone time). I knew that this new year would not bring good things for our family. I knew Mommy could not make it through another one, and I kept asking Neil how we could possibly celebrate the new year when we knew what was coming.

My parents were not having the easiest trip out west either. Mommy felt tired and nauseous most of the time, and Daddy felt sad. As usual, my mother managed to distract herself to try and keep both of their spirits up. Uggs, the Australian sheepskin boots, were all the rage that year and could not be found anywhere on the East Coast. Mommy called me in Massachusetts from her cell phone in Utah. I could barely hear her, but I managed to tell her my preference in color and size through broken cellular signals. While Daddy was out skiing one day, Mommy found the trendy boots in the Stein Eriksen Lodge gift shop. She arrived home a few days later proudly carrying the light pink size 8 Uggs by her side. This made her feel good.

CR

January of 2004 brought about my thirtieth birthday. I wanted to keep the celebration to a minimum, as I was not in such a celebratory mood. Jonny and Jill's wedding was just two weeks away. I was actually starting to believe that we could get there. I felt an enormous sense of relief.

Neil arranged a mini surprise birthday party weekend for me in New York City with lots of my friends in attendance. I smiled through it all as everyone inquired about the health of my mother. "Thank you for asking," was the response I had learned to give. I did not want to lie and say that she was just fine, and I did not want to get into it with everyone. This was a family issue. I spoke of it only to a few very dear friends.

On my actual birthday, my mother rallied through the severe pains in her stomach to spend the day with me in Newtown. Part of her birthday present to me was a sitter for the baby. She never missed a beat. We had lunch at one of our favorite local places. I watched closely as Mommy pushed around the grilled chicken on her plate. Nothing seemed to stick with her. She took her Kytril as if it were aspirin and chased it down with flat ginger ale.

After lunch, we headed over to Angel Heart for that special gift. Mommy wanted it to be long-lasting, but not too old-looking like some of my grandmother's antique jewelry. Margie, one of the saleswomen at Angel Heart, showed us magnificent tourmaline chandelier earrings with a matching necklace. I thought that the earrings would have been enough, but Mommy insisted on getting me the necklace as well. "I'll borrow it from you sometime," she said. "Don't worry." I knew that she never would. She had Margie wrap up the earrings and necklace so that she could give them to me later the next night at the actual birthday celebration.

CR

We had made it to the wedding and back. Everything went smoothly. Jonny and Jill were so happy together, and I was so happy for them. They deserved their day, and they finally got it. Everyone in attendance fought back their tears on the night of the wedding as they watched Mommy dance with Jonny—a bit slower than usual, and with her protruding stomach and somewhat jaundiced skin. I spent a lot of time in the bathroom that night splashing water on my face and telling myself to enjoy the evening as much as I could. We were getting fewer and fewer of them.

As spring approached, Dr. Sato felt that the treatments, even in the more aggressive format, were not effective. He suggested injecting chemotherapy directly into Mommy's liver. This was not good news, but we knew that we would not be getting good news again. Mommy, however, managed to look on the bright side of things. As long as the doctors could do something, Mommy had hope. Her worst nightmare was for them to send her home with no options. Dr. Sato knew this, and we trusted him enough to know that he would never do that.

One of the side effects of the injected chemotherapy was hair loss. This is a reality that many cancer patients face, and we felt lucky that Mommy did not have to think about this, until now—almost six years into living with cancer. Knowing that Mommy would most likely lose her hair, Aunt Jo took her down to the wig store in Cherry Hill, New Jersey. I could not go with them since I had gone back to work part-time after having the baby, something that my mother was so proud of. "You are not to be my nurse. You have a wonderful family and a career, and you go about your business," she told me.

This was by far the hardest shopping trip Aunt Jo had to venture on with her sister. They spent a lot of time at the store selecting one wig made of real hair that looked identical to her own and a synthetic wig that Mommy thought she could wear under hats and with headbands.

Mommy called me at work from the car on the way home. "We found the most beautiful wigs. I will use the real one when I have to, but the cutest one is the fake one. I'll wear it with all my baseball hats and with the new Pucci scarves that I just bought. Will you come over with the baby tonight so I can show you?" "Great," I replied. "I can't wait to see everything. I'll bring over some cute barrettes for them." It was so hard to maintain a stiff upper lip through this conversation. I could hear the fear masked by a smile in her voice, and I did my best to follow along. I hung up the phone and wept out loud in my office. Finally, the tears could come no more, so I blew my nose and went back to work just as Mommy wanted.

◌౩

The wigs were now a staple in my mother's wardrobe. She told everyone about them, and they all said that they couldn't tell. I honestly believe that they were telling the truth. As in the case of all her accessories, Mommy had good wigs. One warm spring day, I met Aunt Jo and Mommy at the Velvet Slipper in Newtown. I had just finished a baby music class with Joey in town, and they were shopping for spring shoes. When I arrived at the store, Mommy was sitting down on the bench, and she looked very weak. She flashed her big toothy smile to Joey and me as she showed off some fancy flip-flops that she thought I would like. At this point, I couldn't even think about wearing new clothes or shoes. I wondered if she would ever see me in any of these new purchases. I ended up getting a pair of pink and green ones. Mommy could not even stand up to hand Carol, the store's owner, her credit card.

I thanked Mommy as Aunt Jo got a glass of water for her. Aunt Jo did not think Mommy was well enough to drive home by herself, so she drove her home in Mommy's car. I followed them and then drove Aunt Jo back into town to pick up her car. All the while, baby Joey slept in the backseat. He was always such a good baby, in large part due to the fact that he had to be. I was a calm mother because I had to be a nervous daughter.

Mommy thanked us for the ride home and attributed her weakness to the chemotherapy. At this point, it could have been from anything. I put the new shoes away in my closet thinking that I could never wear them, as they would always remind me of the sad day. Sure enough, Mommy called that night to give me some suggestions of upcoming events that I could wear them to.

CR

Mommy took me to the Philadelphia Flower Show that spring. She had gone almost every year with her mother, but I had never been. Part of the treat included a babysitter, so I drove Mommy down to Philadelphia. We had a fun lunch at the Reading Terminal Market, followed by handmade chocolates for dessert. Mommy and I had both inherited our sweet tooth from Padee. I was happy to see her with an appetite for chocolate that day. After wandering through the intricate flower displays across the street at the convention center, we headed back home. As Mommy said, "This was just enough."

My mother's cell phone rang in the car. It was Aunt Jo, and she was at Priorities for Her in Newtown holding some sweaters that had just come in. She thought they would be perfect for Mommy. My mother's spirits lifted immediately. She popped another Kytril and directed me to the store. Mommy tried on several of the brightly colored spring sweaters. Aunt Jo had preselected all size large or extra large for the bloated stomach. I tried not to stare at her growing yellow stomach and shrinking chest and rear end. The tumors had taken over, so that my mother's body was no longer her own. She bought about five sweaters that day. It did not matter that she had no place to go in them. It was the thought that she could go somewhere in them that kept her going.

On that same shopping trip, we picked out spring clothes for me—capri pants, skirts, and tops. Mommy and Aunt Jo watched as I tried on the items. They told me that everything looked adorable. I felt guilty for having my own slim, healthy body. I would have given anything to make Mommy's tumors go away. This was the bargaining stage of grief, I had learned—it did no good. These were ridiculous thoughts, and I tried to banish them from my head. Mommy was so happy to buy me things, so happy that I looked good in them, and so happy that I had places to go in them. "Aunt Jo will take you for fall clothes," she said. I gave Mommy a big hug and a kiss. "We'll all go together," I replied.

CR

Aunt Jo was now working overtime to keep Mommy occupied and happy. She took her up to Hedy Shepard's in Princeton to take a look at their new spring tops. At this point, new pants were out of the question. She was so bloated that she wore only a few old black pants that fit below the abdomen.

As usual, modesty was not an issue with my mother. She took off her wig in front of the ladies who worked in the store. It was easier to try on things that way. No one said a word as my bald and bloated mother searched through sweater sets that she hoped would flatter her. Even Aunt Jo was amazed at the way she carried herself that day and at the number of clothes she purchased. Many of those items remained in her closet with the tags still on.

Aunt Jo helped Mommy down the steps and held her shopping bags as they left the store. "It was so nice to see you two out together this afternoon," said Lynne, the owner of the store and a family friend. The sisters knew that they had a special relationship, and they didn't need anyone to remind them. They headed across the street to the Carousel Diner, where Mommy ate half of her grilled cheese sandwich. At this point, she would eat anything that would stay down.

CR

Even in the final weeks of her life, Mommy continued to buy things for the future. She needed something to look forward to. She needed the normalcy. After a restless night's sleep followed by a lazy morning in bed, Mommy drove down the street to her friend Inez's house. Mommy would not go far by herself.

Inez ran a stationery business from home. Mommy noticed that she was running out of note cards, so she made a date to order some more. After looking through books and books of cards, Mommy selected a white card with pink and green flowers that said "Becky" in bubbly handwriting. Although her real name was Rebecca, everyone called her Becky. Rebecca seemed too grownup even for this ailing fifty-seven-year-old. Mommy ordered one hundred cards. Inez took the order that day, but she didn't have the heart to place it. She requested only fifty from the manufacturer, and Mommy never knew the difference.

# CHAPTER 8

I N EARLY JUNE, Mommy called me up one morning and announced that she had to take me on an errand. Figuring that she needed something at a store and therefore needed my opinion, I picked her up later that day. She directed me to the Wachovia Bank in Yardley. "I don't want you to be upset," she said, "but I want to give you access to all of the jewelry in the safe deposit box." I was a bit startled, though not completely surprised. Earlier in the year, Aunt Jo walked me through the process of getting my own safe deposit box so that when the inevitable came, none of Madee and Mommy's jewelry would get lost in the shuffle.

I showed the proper identification and had my name added to my parents' box. Mommy then took the box out, and we went into a private room together. She proceeded to take out all of the jewelry and explain to me where everything came from. We talked about the amethyst earrings and necklace that Madee had given to her when I was born, the garnet-and-pearl necklace and earrings that Mommy wore to my bat mitzvah and then again to my wedding, Great-Grandma Miller's antique diamond pin and earrings, and the double-strand pearl necklace and matching bracelet with the sapphire heart clasps that were staples at all the parties the girls attended.

"I am not upsetting you, am I?" asked Mommy. Through my teary eyes, I told her how I was sad. "I know, sweetie. You are too young to go through this," she said. "I'm very strong," I managed to mumble out. "I know you are," said Mommy with a hug. She then pulled out Madee's favorite earrings—the antique gold ones with the diamonds in the middle and the fringe on the bottom—along with her slide bracelet, which had been given to her by her parents as a confirmation gift. "Madee wore the earrings to every High Holiday service at the temple, and I did the same with the slide bracelet. I want you to wear them to the funeral—my funeral." I cried and hugged her back. What else could I do?

There was my mother, sick as a dog, yet stronger than anyone I had ever known. It made her feel good still to give instructions up until the end. I complied. On the day of the funeral, I wore the earrings and the bracelet, along with

Madee's charm bracelet, which had been given to me by Padee after his wife had passed away. On that very difficult day, when we laid my mother to rest and my brother and I read the eulogy that Mommy had requested I write, I needed a piece of Madee with me. I needed the strength of all the great women in my life.

☙

My mother selected her final outfit all by herself. For six years, Mommy lived with cancer and lived life to the fullest. For six years, she carried on and never once felt sorry for herself. Only in the last week of her life did the tumors take over so much that she could not get out of bed. We had many wonderful talks in those last few days. If the truth be told, there were no dramatic, tearful deathbed good-byes like the ones I used to watch on *General Hospital.* There were no regrets—nothing was left unsaid throughout our lives. I asked her if she thought we appreciated each moment more since she had been sick. Her response was that we always knew how good we had it. We didn't have to change because of the disease.

Even just days before dying, Mommy did some shopping of her own in her mind's eye. She instructed Aunt Jo to take out her new hooded pink sweater and shell, black pants, and new "fun" Stuart Weitzman shoes. Along with that, she requested the fake jewelry that she bought from her manicurist just the week before and her big floppy Pucci hat that she ordered from Saks over the phone from the confines of her bed. Mommy wanted to be buried in those items. Many people are buried in a formal suit with their grandmother's pearls. Mommy would be laid to rest looking just as she did in life—bright and cheery.

Her friend Roz came by to visit during the last week and gave Mommy a striped pink-and-yellow watch from a catalog that Mommy had admired. At that point, Mommy had slipped into a hepatic coma. Maybe she saw the watch, maybe not. "It was for the journey," Roz said. We placed it on her wrist after she took her last breath. Weeks after the funeral, one of my grandmother's oldest friends told me that my mother came into this world as a lady and left it as a lady. I could not have said it better myself.

CR

I dreaded the call. "Hello, Rebecca [people always confused Rachel with Rebecca], this is Wendy from Calico Corners. I am calling to let you know that your cushions are

ready. You can pick them up at your earliest convenience."
"Thank you," I said and promptly hung up the phone. It
had been four weeks to the day of my mother's funeral. Just
eight weeks prior to that day, Mommy took me to the fabric
store in Yardley to pick out cushions for the furniture in a
room that we had just added to our house.

It was a struggle for Mommy to get to the store that
day. She took a seat while Wendy, the saleswoman who was
helping us, brought fabrics to her. I thought that Wendy
knew that Mommy was sick, but apparently, she attributed
her sweating and nausea to the hot weather (as my mother
did that day). Mommy selected plaids in corals and yellows,
along with off-white cushions with coral-and-green fringe.
I must admit that she had an eye for decorating. When
I look around my house, I see my mother's taste almost
everywhere, and I smile.

I headed down to Calico the day after I received the
phone message, with Joey in the stroller. After playing with
the baby for a while, Wendy casually asked how my mother
was. This was the awkward moment I have now come to
know all too well. "She passed away," I responded. I gave
her the quick "it's not so bad" version of the story because I
really did not feel like opening my heart out to Wendy, the
"I can't add any two plus two without a calculator" cushion

saleslady. "Oh, you must feel terrible that she will not see the baby grow up." *You stupid lady!* I thought. *No, I am actually really excited about that. It wouldn't have been that much fun anyway.* I rolled my eyes. I have learned that if people don't know what to say, they should not say anything at all. I left the store with the cushions in my hand and my heart in my stomach.

∝

Although Mommy had instructed Aunt Jo to take me shopping for fall clothes before she died, I wanted to do it on my own. This may sound silly to some, but walking into one of those stores by myself took a lot of courage. Picture Jackie Kennedy walking into the White House after the assassination. One rainy Saturday afternoon in August, while Neil took the baby up to see his parents, I went to Newtown all by myself. I was greeted with huge hugs and long faces by the entire staff of Priorities for Her. I laughed to myself, remembering what my father had said a few weeks ago. All the shop owners and workers from the stores that my mother had frequented came to her funeral. Daddy joked that they were all probably crying for their livelihoods, as they no longer had their number one customer. Well, maybe number two, behind Aunt Jo.

They all complimented me on the eulogy and told me how much they loved my mother. They would miss seeing us all together. Meanwhile, they knew that Aunt Jo would be moving down to Savannah that winter. Aunt Jo and Uncle Dick had always wanted to retire down there, and now that Aunt Jo had taken care of her parents and her sister until the end, she could go. The saleswomen were genuinely touched by my family and really would miss seeing us together. I appreciated the sentiment, put a smile on my face, and started to shop.

Linda, the store's owner, helped me pick out some great-colored corduroys that had just come in for the fall. I also found several sweaters, some in the year's newest trend of argyle. I could hear my mother right then and there. "I should have saved all my old argyle sweaters. I'd be right in style," she would have said. I also picked out some dressier pants, a short black skirt with lace underneath, and a gray cashmere sweater. These would suit me well for the upcoming High Holidays. I had come a long way from the jumpers Madee used to pick out for me to wear to temple.

I left the store that day feeling relieved and proud. I had done it all by myself, and I survived. Of course, some things would never change. I headed directly to Aunt Jo's house and showed her my purchases. She loved everything. Even more than that, she told me that I really was my own woman who could make her own decisions, and would lead a wonderful life. This was a lot to dissect from just one shopping trip, but I knew what she meant.

CR

Joey's first birthday was just a few months after the funeral. We decided to have a big party. *Life goes on*, I kept saying to myself. Aunt Jo called me up the night before we were going to a luncheon with some of my mother's dear friends. "After lunch, I am taking you to the Children's Clothing Patch to buy Joey a birthday outfit." She could have offered to buy him a paper bag, and I would have cried at that. It was the gesture that counted. We arrived at the children's store that we had so often frequented with Mommy. I could tell that the staff at the store had not heard the news about my mother, but we did not say a word—no need to go there that day.

One of the newer employees helped us sort through the twelve—to eighteen-month-old-boy sizes. We found the perfect party outfit in powder blue pants and a cable-knit top with a white corduroy collar. I knew that Neil would think it was too girly, but it was classic, just as it should be. In the end, Neil knew that it was the right look. Either that, or he just didn't care as much as I did. Joey ended up wearing it for only one hour on the day of the party due to the hot weather and the vanilla icing from the cake.

I continued to browse around the store, and I could see Aunt Jo watching me out of the corner of my eye. She looked on as I felt the fabric of a few overall outfits. She quickly grabbed them out of my hands and took them to the cash register. "We'll take all of these," she emphatically said. "No, no," I insisted. "Rachel, dear—it's my pleasure. I want to do this," Aunt Jo replied. For just one brief moment, I stopped asking myself why my mother wasn't there with me. I felt lucky that my mother had this sister. Then I missed Mommy, again.

ᘉ

I made another trip to the Children's Clothing Patch after the birthday party. This time, my father came along.

He was following up on his promise—he said that he would be the mother and the father. In truth, I just needed him to be himself. Just like Mommy, on that day, he held my hand as we combed through the racks of little-boy clothing. We ended up with overalls, pants, tops, shoes, and a jacket. Daddy had fun picking out the cowboys, the footballs, the stripes, and more.

As he stood at the cash register, I strolled Joey around and came across the Noah's Ark quilt that my mother had bought for Joey a few months ago. "That's the one that Mommy bought," I told my father across the room. I saw the owner of the store shoot a look to one of the employees, and I realized that they weren't sure what had happened to my mother. "I am not sure if you heard the news," I began, "but my mother passed away this summer."

They were so sorry, they did not know, how awful. I found myself comforting other people again—an all-too-familiar occurrence. A week later, I received a beautiful note in the mail from "everyone at the Children's Clothing Patch." It was amazing to me how people who had just seen us shopping together over the years really felt that they knew what we were about. In many ways, they did.

CR

As things began to calm down in the fall, Aunt Jo and I walked into a new store in Princeton. We looked around for a while, then Aunt Jo asked the saleslady a question about one of the scarves. "Your mother has great taste," said the woman. "That is your mother, right?" I felt the blood rush to my face as a million thoughts came into my head. *No, that's not my mother, you idiot. My mother is dead. My mother will never again walk into a store with me. She'll never bring home hair accessories for me just because. She'll never pick out the layette for the next baby, never find me a dress for the holiday party at Neil's office, never help me find the perfect paint color for the finished basement, never have the opportunity to tell me that I am too old for the dress that I am trying on for Joey's bar mitzvah. She won't be there to grow old with my father or see my brother become a father, never help Aunt Jo decorate her new house in Savannah.* I felt so cheated!

Reality sank back in. "That's my aunt." I smiled back at the woman, downplaying this issue. I could see Aunt Jo feel my pain across the store as she looked into my eyes. Blue eyes—just like my mother's. Only, for some reason, the melanoma did not attack my blue eyes or Aunt Jo's green eyes. Then it hit me again for what it seemed like the millionth time—there was no reason. Mommy got the melanoma like someone else gets hit by a car—it was just bad luck. Luck—there was that feeling again. As Mommy said, "You are lucky to have Aunt Jo."

I was lucky for many reasons: for my health, for my father and my brother and my wonderful family and friends, for my life with Neil and Joey, and for all those days with Madee, with Aunt Jo, with Mommy.

I will walk into a countless number of stores again. It will get easier—that is what they say, and I believe them. In so many ways, however, they made it easy on me. In every one of those stores, I hear Madee telling me to stand up straight, Aunt Jo telling me that I look like a lampshade, and Mommy, my beautiful, dear, wonderful mommy, asking me where I am going in that. Lots of places.

# EPILOGUE

YOU NEVER KNOW when it's going to hit you. My mother has been dead for three years. For three years, I have avoided the card aisle in the grocery store in early May, nervous that the sight of a Shoebox Mother's Day card, which used to make me laugh out loud, would bring me to tears. Three Jewish New Years have passed, where I eat apples and honey at the kitchen counter by myself. I used to love to eat apples and honey out of the cream-and-gold china honeybee at my mother's beautifully set dining room table while she would plant a kiss on my forehead, wishing me a sweet new year. Three fall and three spring lines of clothing have come and gone through the stores without my mother getting a peek at any of them. Mommy will never know about the return of the tunic, the poncho, or even the once-dreaded leggings. Skinny jeans would mean nothing to her. She'll never get to see how the maternity toggle sweater with the patches on the elbows was one of the best purchases I have made—pregnant or not pregnant.

People call me on her birthday or the anniversary of her death. They ask if I've been to the cemetery. They are thinking of her today. I think of her every day. In all honesty, I feel the same on her birthday as I do the day after. I have been to the cemetery only three times. Once with my uncle, who showed me how to get there; a second time for the unveiling, where I was more concerned with my baby son, who was fussy in his stroller; and a third time to see if I could survive a visit by myself. I did, and it didn't hit me.

Then it hit me. On the way to the playground with my two young children buckled into their car seats, I reached through the open car window into the mailbox to pick up the oversized envelope that was shoved in between a few bills and catalogs. The return address was unfamiliar. What was in it was not—a pink-and-purple polka dot Baby Lulu cotton dress with a ruffled skirt. I knew I had seen this dress before, and I never forget a pretty outfit. The card inside jogged my memory. It was addressed to my baby daughter, Rebecca. She was born a year and a half after my mother died, and she was named after my mother, Becky. I was at first confused as I read the note.

Dear Rebecca,

Welcome to the world! When I was born, your Grandma Becky sent me this adorable little outfit. I wore it over the summer, and always got compliments on how cute I looked. When we heard that you were born, we decided that you should have this outfit because we knew that your Grandma thought it was perfect for a little girl and would want you to look as cute as I did. I hope you enjoy it and know that your Grandma Becky picked it out herself.

Love,

Rachel (and Lauren too)

    I was with my mother when she bought the Baby Lulu dress for our family friend's new baby daughter, Rachel. I remembered that day. I remembered thinking that the name *Rachel*, my name, would never go out of style. None of the biblical ones do. I remembered finding the Baby Lulu dress from the new spring arrivals box at the Children's Clothing Patch. My mother was having some trouble on that Indian summer day in early December. She was wearing her new hooded sweater coat that she bought with her sister the week before. The fur-lined trim collar was making her hot, and she was tired from her latest targeted chemotherapy treatment. I remembered the satisfied smile on her face after she realized that this was a great baby gift—much better than a hooded towel and a bib, or worse, another blanket. This was a dress that a little girl should wear.

And now my daughter would get to wear it. Like the note said, "your Grandma Becky picked it out herself." I was happy that Rebecca would have one piece of clothing selected by my mother. Then I was sad—only one. In a million years, I never would have imagined that my mother would not know my children. I have a little girl to shop for, but no one left to shop for me.